A Fish

by Wan Lee • illustrated by Becka Moor

"Look at this sad fish. This fish has a wish. What is she wishing?"

"I wish I was a ship! A ship is big and fast. That ship is the best!"

"I wish I was a king! That king has a big ring. That king can sing!"

"I wish I was a moth! These moths have wings. These moths can flit and fly!"

"Could I fly like a moth? No, but I can jump! Look, is this a fish?"

"I wish I was a fish! A fish has fins and gills. A fish can jump and swim!"

"Look at our pal now. This fish is glad. She is glad to be a fish!"